Marketing

The Top 100 Best Things That You Can Do In Order To Make Money & Be Successful With Marketing

By Ace McCloud
Copyright © 2014

Disclaimer

The information provided in this book is designed to provide helpful information on the subjects discussed. This book is not meant to be used, nor should it be used, to diagnose or treat any medical condition. For diagnosis or treatment of any medical problem, consult your own physician. The publisher and author are not responsible for any specific health or allergy needs that may require medical supervision and are not liable for any damages or negative consequences from any treatment, action, application or preparation, to any person reading or following the information in this book. Any references included are provided for informational purposes only. Readers should be aware that any websites or links listed in this book may change.

Table of Contents

Introduction 6

Chapter 1: Business Identity – Branding, Logos and Customer Service 8

Chapter 2: Determining Your Target Market Audience 13

Chapter 3: Prospecting: How to Find Your Customers and Keep Them Coming Back For More 16

Chapter 4: How To Be Successful With Social Media Marketing 24

Chapter 5: The Best Sales Techniques for Marketing 32

Chapter 6: Marketing Secrets That Help Drive Sales & Profit 36

Conclusion 42

My Other Books and Audio Books 43

DEDICATED TO THOSE WHO ARE PLAYING THE GAME OF LIFE TO

WIN

KEEP ON PUSHING AND NEVER GIVE UP!

Ace McCloud

4

Be sure to check out my website for all my Books and Audio books.
www.AcesEbooks.com

Introduction

I want to thank you and congratulate you for buying the book: "Marketing: The Top 100 Best Things That You Can Do In Order To Make Money And Be Successful With Marketing."

There are two main factors when it comes to running a successful business—marketing and sales. Marketing is the backbone of sales in any business because it helps you bring in fresh prospects that good sales tactics can turn into customers. Without customers, businesses can't make any money and without good customer relationships, people will not purchase your product or service or refer people to your business. When it comes down to it, marketing is what lets people know that your business exists. If nobody knows about your business, you will never make money, no matter how awesome your product or services are. Marketing is also important for boosting brand awareness, gaining valuable market place knowledge; ideas for strategically marketing your business, along with many other valuable things that will help your business thrive.

Without proper marketing, it is more than likely that a business will fail within a few months. Marketing, while useful and effective, is also a very broad topic. It covers many subtopics, such as social media marketing, business development and much more that you will discover in this book. With that being said, small businesses often view marketing as daunting and overwhelming. There are many different types and styles of marketing as well as different strategies that you can use to make your business spread like wildfire. The right combination of all marketing types can give your business a powerful boost and help drive sales and leads to your front door. Though you will have to make some investments for certain marketing strategies to work, the return is often well worth the initial investment.

To be successful in marketing and sales, you will have to establish a brand for your business. You will then have to master everything from customer service to identifying your target audience to creating ideal customer profiles to increasing your presence online to picking out the best strategies that work best for you. It can be an extremely overwhelming process! Many people think that all marketers need a degree, but that's not true—anyone can do it and you will discover just how easy it can be in this book.

This book contains proven steps and strategies on how you can become a master marketer. You will discover the secrets to every aspect of marketing while learning from some of the best industry leaders in the world, including life lessons from Starbucks, Kodak, Coca-Cola and more. Most importantly, you will discover some of the best and easiest to implement secrets and strategies for acquiring customers. Near the end of this book is a marketing action plan where you can review everything you've learned and put it all together for a personally developed action plan for your ultimate success. Whether you are just starting out or if you're already a business owner who is just looking to extend your brand, customer base, or knowledge, this book will guide you along the right path so that you can become a marketing expert and proceed forward with a successful and profitable business!

Chapter 1: Business Identity – Branding, Logos and Customer Service

Branding is important for any business because it allows your business to develop an identity, both on and offline. It leaves your audience with an impression of what your business is and how you run things. There are many benefits to branding that cannot be missed. First, when people see you as an expert, it helps strengthen your brand. Second, it can help your business attract like-minded people, who may become a valued customer or partner. Third and very importantly, it can help you build a strong reputation in your field. For example, look at fast food—you've probably heard of little-name restaurants here and there, but everyone in the USA knows the three big leaders: McDonalds, Wendy's and Burger King. That is mostly due to the way those companies have developed their brand.

Planning Your Brand

Before you can develop your brand, you have to plan it. This will take some personal thought and reflection on your part. The best thing to do would be to set some goals for yourself in terms of branding your business. Ask yourself a few questions such as:

- Do you want to attract like-minded clients and/or potential business partners?

- Do you want your company to develop a solid reputation?

- What message do you want to get across to your audience?

- What does your company stand for?

- What do you want others to say about your business?

Those are just some common questions, be sure to rack your mind and answer as many questions as you can in regards to your business and brand. Then, take the five – ten most important things and turn them into a goal for your business that you can work towards. Be sure to put the most important goals first, and it is always a good idea to start off each goal with the phrase: "I will easily..."

The Big Branding Secret

The big secret to establishing a successful brand is to make it about you. Yes, you heard right—make it about you. Now, that doesn't mean to become egotistical and to put your face on your company's logo. What it *does* mean is to give it a personal touch. For example, Starbucks is commonly perceived as "coffee for snobs" due to its upscale environment, vast selection of drinks and its slightly bigger price tag. However, the CEO of the company, Howard Schultz, goes into deep detail about the Starbuck's brand in his book "Onward."

In one part of the book, he talks about how he went to another country and entered a coffee shop. In that coffee shop, the workers poured the coffee like artwork right in front of the customer, not like you would usually see if you went to an American coffee shop and just ordered your coffee and got it. He decided to bring that touch back to the states with him, along with the "feel" of those shops, and thus Starbucks was born. He even put a vast amount of effort into the way the coffee was made (with freshly ground beans for every cup, every day) to the equipment that the company used. Starbucks could have been like any old corner coffee shop, but Howard Schultz wanted to share his personal experience with coffee with his audience. That is why Starbucks is so successful today.

Another key strategy is to build a fan base. Think about a celebrity whom you admire. Surely you've rented and bought their movies, downloaded their songs, read their books or have supported their endeavors in some way financially. Why do you think that happened? It most likely wasn't a random act of kindness—you did that because you support and like that person. One of your goals is to build a fan base just like that. The more fans you have (which translates to the more people you can touch, inspire and make happy), the more successful your brand is likely to be. Think about it some more... there's always a key player for every medium who has fans. Lots of people love the New England Patriots football team, but even more people go crazy over the quarterback Tom Brady.

Here are some really good ways to build a fan base:

- Connect with people who share your beliefs.

- Try to entertain people if you can.

- Connect with people through your personal experiences.

- Inspire your audience.

- Attract people through your personality.

If you're attractive, it can be a good idea to take advantage of that. If not, there are hundreds of other ways to build a great fan base. Experiment with some of these strategies to see if you can become a respectable and reputable person in your industry.

Presenting Your Brand

The way you present your brand is a key step in building fans, loyal customers and success. By coming up with an excellent presentation, you are essentially getting into the minds of your buyers. The key is to remember to focus on your buyers. Your company logo may have special meaning to you, but what does it mean to consumers? The best way to come up with the best presentation of your brand ever is to put yourself in the shoes of your audience—what would attract them to your business? Here are a few things to consider when building the presentation of your brand:

- What does the name of your company mean to your audience? What does it reflect?

- Is your website address accessible and easy to remember?

- How does your product or service directly benefit your audience?

- Does your competition have any weaknesses and can you take advantage of them?

For example, my company slogan is: "The Best E-Books At The Best Price." In that one sentence people can easily determine that I am providing extremely high quality books at an incredible price!

Another good example comes from Kodak. Think about Kodak and "Kodak moments." Kodak came up with the term "Kodak moments" to describe moments in time that people would want to capture forever using a camera made by that company. A typical "Kodak moment" is something cute, memorable and/or something that one would want to treasure. For example, a young couple might have their baby and their puppy playing together and the dad might chuckle, "What a Kodak moment!" So even if that couple wasn't using a Kodak brand camera, the mentioning of the brand still occurred. Watch this commercial, Kodak Commercial – The Kodak Moment – 1993 to see what they did and try and use it as an example as to what you can try and do for your product or service.

A really good way to start looking for marketing ideas is to put yourself in the shoes of your audience and then brainstorm some ideas on their beliefs or on what they would want. The key is to focus on your target audiences beliefs because people will tend to follow what they perceive is true. Of course, when it comes to branding and presentation, always try to make yourself stand out. With the thousands of industries out there today, it can be really easy to fit in with the crowd. Your goal is to stand out. You can do this by focusing on things that are specific about you. For example, many people can be a freelance writer, but maybe you're a freelance writer who has a really fast work ethic. You could brand yourself as "fast" and "reliable" and that may help you attract more clients. Think of it as a hook phrase that will attract and help keep customers.

Customer Service and Your Brand

Customer service is something that most consumers dread because it is often a lengthy and frustrating process. Usually it involves complications, communication problems, long wait times and overall dissatisfaction, which often leads to a person never buying from a particular company again. When you have a business, offering above and beyond customer service can help you boost your brand identity and create customers for life. When you have great customer service, people will be much more likely to tell others about their great experience with you, which counts as some free marketing and bonus customers in the future.

One of the best known cases in brand building with customer service is about the online shoe company Zappos. Now, you can buy shoes practically anywhere, and the CEO knew that the company needed a way to stand out. The executive team at Zappos figured out that one of the biggest issues with buying shoes online would be returns. Knowing that returns would be complex as well as costly, Zappos created a customer service policy that included free shipping and a return policy that was as hassle-free as possible. Additionally, the employees in the customer service department weren't given specific directions on what to say during disputes—rather, they were instructed to do whatever it took to make the customer happy. Legend has it that one customer service employee spent 8 hours helping a customer on the phone. Due to Zappos' extraordinary customer service department, the company was able to accumulate $1 billion in sales within 10 years and customers spread the word about the company like crazy.

For small businesses, it is important to instill the "the customer is always right" motto in its employees. Anyone who has worked a low-level job has probably thought to themselves at one point, "the customer is NOT always right!" Even if it is true in some cases, it is crucial to just go by the original saying. The better your business can treat a customer, the more likely they are to become a loyal customer for life. When it comes down to it, it is generally best to treat customers the way that you would want your favorite business to treat you. Even if having a strong customer service department costs you some money and effort, (training, staffing, replacement products, etc.), you can be sure that the investment will pay off in the long run. As everyone knows, in business and in your personal life, reputation is everything.

Zappos' customer service story was big in the early 2000's, when the company first launched. Now customer service is an even a bigger opportunity thanks to social media. Many businesses have "fan pages" on Facebook, Twitter, and other social media platforms, all of which customers can access and interact with. Customer service is just as important as ever because now an angry customer can easily go on to your Facebook page and write something like, "I had such a bad experience with the customer service department, they gave me such a hard time when I was trying to return this product, and I vow to never shop with this company again!" and guess what—all of the followers of that page will see it! This is why customer service is so very important these days. There are even a variety of websites, such as Angie's list, which are totally devoted to customers who want to express their opinions about a particular product or company.

It is said that people are twice as likely to post a bad review as they are to post a good review. However, it is very possible for a company to get nothing but good reviews (for the most part). Look around on Facebook for some popular business pages. Compare and contrast to see what's going on. If you notice a business is getting a lot of complaints via their page, try to find some patterns and clues as to why this might be happening. If you find a page that is getting nothing but excellent comments and reviews, also try to see if you can figure out what they're doing differently. This could be a good company to model yourself after.

All in all, never be afraid to go above and beyond with your customer service. Do something extra nice for your customers and you will likely get hundreds of customers for life over time. Don't be afraid to be creative—think outside the box and do something that will make you stand out from the hundreds of businesses in your field!

Chapter 2: Determining Your Target Market Audience

Your target market audience is the specific group of people that you will be advertising your product or services too. The point of having a target market audience is to narrow your focus while boosting your sales. Many people make the mistake of trying to market their business to "anybody and everybody" with the hopes of reaching as many consumers as possible. While it seems like the easy way out, it's actually one of the worst strategies you could have. Targeting a specific, narrowed niche can help you boost sales in many ways. First, you'll be interacting with people who actually need your product or service. They will be like-minded people and you will have the upper hand in "getting into their mind." This chapter will go into business development and how you can define your target market audience to get the best results as well as how to grow your consumer base.

Developing a Business Development Strategy

With a business development strategy you will bring together all aspects of sales and marketing to determine when and how to reach out to new consumers. Creating a business development strategy is a process that should be worked on carefully, as it requires extensive planning, progression and implementation of different types of goals. In creating your development strategy, you can define your target market audience.

The Five W's of Your Target Market Audience

To get started, it can be helpful to answer these five questions:

- Who are you targeting?

- What are you selling to these targets?

- Where are your targets located?

- When will you approach your targets?

- Why would your targets be interested in your business?

- How will you reach your targets?

Let's break this down with a real business example. Take Nintendo—one of the leading video game companies in the world. Nintendo's "who" is children and their families. What makes them stand out from Sony and Microsoft is that Nintendo puts out more "family-friendly" video games—their "what." Although Nintendo is a worldwide company, they have a branch called Nintendo of

America—that's their "where." The "when" part can be tricky, but a good way to show this for Nintendo is in their holiday advertisement. When Nintendo printed their magazine, Nintendo Power, they used to send out a huge special edition right before Christmas that cataloged all of their best games in hopes that kids would ask their parents to buy those games for them for Christmas. For their "how", Nintendo markets themselves on different platforms. It has various social media accounts, including Facebook and Twitter as well as a website and an online platform that is accessible through their consoles. They also reach their targets through merchandising, such as stuffed animal versions of their video game heroes, action figures, books, etc. They used to have a magazine but faded it out after social media took over.

Planning Out Your Business

The planning process is the most important part of your business development and marketing plan because it requires a lot of thinking. The first half of a successful business requires planning while the last half requires action. To make it easy on yourself, just start at the top and work your way to the end.

I've found that the most effective way to plan your business is to forecast the entire year and then revise it as you move from quarter to quarter. Again, you can ask yourself the following set of questions to get started on planning:

- Where is your business today?

- Where should your business be in the next four months?

- What needs to be done differently, if anything?

- What specific things need to be done to reach your next goal(s)?

- Are there any barriers to your goals?

- What will the results bring?

Answer each question specifically so that it can serve as your guide. Most importantly, answering these questions every quarter can help you keep your business and goals on track. The best way to conduct this is to open a new word document and paste these questions into five separate pages: one for your forecast and four for each quarter. Go back to this document at the start of every quarter to review and revise your answers. You may also want to take a personal assessment each quarter. This can be helpful because it can help you identify any areas of improvement that you need to make in yourself or your company. This is vitally important, as there is almost nothing worse than making a poor choice or decision for week after week month after month and year after year! Be sure to try to find flaws or areas of improvement that you can fix up and do better in for the future.

Finally, if you have been in business for a few years, you can try another useful strategy: use the past to plan your future. Look at the past decisions and actions of your business and analyze them to determine whether you need to improve or make changes. Always remember that no matter how small, an adjustment can lead to great improvements in the long run! Be sure to automate as many things as possible in your business and always keep an eye out for new ideas, products, or services that can improve your business.

Brainstorming Activity: The Top 25 Reasons Why People Would Want to Buy From YOU!

As this chapter comes to a close, I want you to take some time to brainstorm the top 25 reasons why your target market audience would want to buy from you. You may want to add this list to the document where you have your yearly forecast, quarterly plans and ideal customer profile so that you have it all in one place. Take as much time as you need and think about the things you've learned in this chapter. If you're serious about being successful, don't be lazy at this point! The real winners in life will do these exercises to the best of their ability the first time around and save themselves a lot of pain and heartache in the future! Here are a few more things to consider as you write these reasons down:

- People will buy things to fulfill their needs...think about peoples' basics needs, such as food, shelter, love, etc.

- Does your product or service offer convenience?

- Can your product or service replace something old and serve as an upgrade? (Think about the shift from cassette to CD to mp3)

- Is your product or service considered scarce or valuable?

- Can your product or service offer prestige or otherwise boost the self-esteem of consumers?

- Can you use emotion to get your consumers to buy?

- How will your product or service bring value to your audience?

- Does your company stand for something that will make your consumers feel good about themselves when they make a purchase?

Chapter 3: Prospecting: How to Find Your Customers and Keep Them Coming Back For More

Finding customers or clients can be hard, especially if you're a relatively new business. It can be even more challenging if your budget for marketing is small. The good news is that it is pretty easy to start finding new customers and clients once you discover the best strategies. This chapter will help you find those secrets along with great tips on how to get the most out of them. I think you will be quite surprised to find out how your current clients can help you drive sales.

Finding New Customers and Clients

This is usually where general advertising comes in. When a business has just started and doesn't have a single customer, they instantly start to think about getting the word out. There have been many instances where I have seen new local businesses standing on the street corners handing out fliers, taking out ads in the newspaper, or hanging up signs on community bulletin boards. I've even seen one coffee shop make one of their employees stand out front dressed in a coffee cup costume to attract new customers.

While general advertising as well as brand building is important for attracting customers and retaining them, there are a few more specific strategies that you can use to quicken the process and give yourself the upper edge.

One of the best strategies for finding new customers that I've read about is "host-beneficiary" relationships. With this strategy, a new business usually pairs up with a more established, bigger business that has a similar target audience. The new business will then offer a free gift (usually their product or service) through clients of the established business. This strategy benefits both businesses because current clients of the established business will get something nice from them (at no cost to that business) and the new business will get exposure by providing that product or service as the gift. One clothing business successfully did this by giving away a free silk shirt to any female customer of a local car dealership. The customer would bring a proof of purchase letter from the dealer into the clothing store and get their free shirt—and then often ended up spending more of their own money.

Another really good strategy is networking. While networking might not immediately get you new customers, it *can* land you referrals, which will then generate new customers in the future. Earlier I mentioned teaming up with other professionals in your field to start a referral chain. Talking with people and getting to know others is also a good idea because you never know where opportunity will come from. Networking takes time and will definitely not get you new customers overnight, but the payoff can be amazing if you are consistent with it and find the right business partners! Just try to make it a habit to network with people more and really brush up on your communication skills to make a memorable impression. The better the impression you can make, the more likely people are to remember you and your business.

Cold-calling is an old method to get new customers and even though it can be very challenging, it is still a time-tested method. Unfortunately, it can be easy to give up on cold-calling just because most people know why you're calling—to get their business. Before using this method, I'd recommend brushing up on your communication skills and learn how to build rapport—then give cold-calling a try. In the end, remember these two things—don't take it personally if you get hung up on or if you don't get any leads and never give up! Set goals for yourself and keep going until you literally can't think of anyone else to call! Check out this YouTube video, No Fear Cold Calling, by Gavin Ingham for some more awesome tips on how to nail cold calls. I have personally had incredible success with cold calling back when I was in the mortgage business. The success rate was only one to three percent, but the rewards were huge overtime. It's not always the most enjoyable thing to do, but if things are slow, it can be a great use of your time.

One way to get new customers after you've already established a solid customer base is to start switching up your marketing techniques. In a few chapters you will learn plenty of awesome ways to market your business, so don't be afraid to experiment and/or try them all out at different times. Switching it up could definitely attract new customers. Experimenting this way will also help you figure out what works and what doesn't. This is vitally important. ***To succeed as a business you need to know the best ways to spend your time and money in order to maximize your results!***

Another strategic idea is to offer a new or improved product that could bring on another group of customers to your business. For example, AOL (America Online) got many more customers when it offered a kid-friendly version of the internet many years ago. Another example is when Coke came out with the soda caps that required a "match" to open—this YouTube video, Coca-Cola Friendly Twist by Coca-Cola. Basically, Coke came out with a new type of soda cap that you cannot open unless you find someone who has the same type of cap. When my friend first saw this commercial, she joked, "they just want you to buy two" and although she was just trying to be funny, she was actually kind of right—for Coke, this meant double sales, but for the consumers, this meant fun, discovery, curiosity and something different. Coke's closest competitor, Pepsi, did not have an idea like this, so it even opened the opportunity for loyal Pepsi drinkers to try the new Coke cap.

Acquiring More Business From Your Current Consumers

This part is especially helpful to small businesses that may have a harder time finding leads. However, when done strategically, any kind of company can use this method. This section will talk about the secrets that come straight from the customers you have now. It costs fifteen times as much in time and resource to acquire a brand new client out of nowhere. Many businesses do not realize their real untapped opportunities—current clients.

It's a fairly simple process. Most of it just requires good communication skills and increasing your likeability. First and foremost, keep in touch with your current clients. Treat them as good friends and make them feel important to your business. There is a theory called "The Rule of 52," which states that everybody that you know knows at least 52 other people who can become potential clients. Those 52 people each know an additional 52 people, and so forth. Send out reminders that you're thinking of these clients—most people expect you to be selling them something when you give them a call or email, but if you get in touch to just "say hi" or "see how they're doing," it's going to dramatically boost your rapport. If you have many clients, it can be a good idea to make a list of your very best ones and really focus on building your relationships with them.

There is a pretty straightforward process to gain loyal clients called "The Loyalty Ladder," a well-known strategy in the world of marketing. This ladder is meant to serve as a guide on how clients will interact with you at different stages. "Anybody and everybody, everywhere" starts at the bottom. The second stage is when you pick out those who have a need—one that your business can fulfill. Once you've found those prospects, the next step is to turn them into customers—people who will buy from your business—but they may still buy from your competition as well. Once you've acquired customers, the next step is to turn them into a client—also known as a person who will exclusively do business with you and no one else. Finally, the goal is to turn those clients into advocates of your business. Advocates are the ones who will actually bring in more clients to you through referrals.

Creating Your Ideal Customer Profile

Once you've gotten this far, I am confident that you've got a good grasp on your business, where you're going with it and how you're going to start marketing. At this point, you can now create your ideal customer—a profile that you will use to find the best customers ever. Having this profile on hand can help you easily identify potential clients and it can be helpful information to pass on to your advocates.

Creating this profile is ultimately all up to you, but here are few things to think about when putting it together:

- Think about the industry you're in and how you can use that to your advantage.

- Think about the geographic and demographic characteristics of your ideal customer—this can be useful for marketing.

- Think about the financial trends among your target audience.

18

- Look for customers with good attitudes.

- Come back to this profile every quarter and see how you can improve it.

All in all, don't be afraid to "research" your ideal customer or client. Go to great lengths to figure out what they need, what they want and how they want it. Find out everything you can about them, including what they read, what they watch on TV and what they look for on the internet. Don't be afraid to ask your customers what they want out of you and your business. Some of the most successful businesses of all times have actively questioned their customers and then made improvements and changes based on their feedback. Most of all, don't forget to make your customers feel special!

How to Market To Your Prospective Customers

Now that you've discovered the secrets of how to attract new customers and how to get more out of your current ones, it is time to learn a little more about the actual marketing strategies that can attract and hold your consumers. Get ready for some incredible information! I am about to present a lot of ideas, so it wouldn't be a bad idea for you to get out some paper and take some notes on these marketing strategies.

Common Types of Marketing

You are surely familiar with the most common types of marketing:

- Snail Mail
- Telemarketing
- Showcases
- Seminars
- Email Marketing
- Social media
- Newspaper (articles, advertisements, classifieds, etc)
- Magazines
- TV
- Radio
- Yellow pages
- Billboards
- Catalogs

One thing you should know is that most of these "types" of marketing actually fall into the category of "advertising," which is completely different. Advertising is putting the notice of your product's existence out there and waiting for customers to come to you. Many people in the marketing industry call this "spray and pray advertising, meaning that you put your business out there and then just wait.

The problem with this type of advertising is that it doesn't hold the attention span of most consumers and it can also get expensive—especially if you're printing up the same catalog and just sending it out at random. Even if you go the email route, which is less expensive, it can still give your company a bad reputation and put you in most peoples' spam folder unless you are providing something valuable.

A better way to go is to use narrowcasted marketing. This marketing strategy is deeper and more specific, one in which you actively try to engage with your customers to get the most of your relationship with them. Narrowcasted marketing involves focusing on your target audience and your ideal customer profile. It can also make your business look like an industry leader and it can open the door for opportunities between you and your consumers.

Specific Narrowcasted Marketing Strategies, Techniques, and Ideas

Put Consumers in Control. Control is a powerful thing to have. Who doesn't love being in control of things, especially when most peoples' lives seem to be out of control. By marketing your product or service as something that can give your consumer a sense of control, it may serve as a powerful selling point. In general, people like to be in control of their finances, personal safety, health, jobs, relationships and self-esteem. Furthermore, selling insurance on your product or service can also give the consumer of sense of control. Think about the last time you purchased an expensive item (maybe a new laptop or a set of new tires for your car) and you were asked if you wanted to pay extra for insurance purposes. People like knowing that they can get the most support out of their buck. If your product or service can provide consumers with a sense of control, it can be a very powerful idea to market it under that category. Also, this strategy works particularly well for products that perform well and rarely have significant problems with them.

Get Them Through Their Family Values. Family is something that the majority of people value in life. For example, think about Disney World: people go to that theme park for rides, food, games and more, but what distinguishes Disney World from any theme park? The difference is that many people think of Disney world as a place to spend time with family. There is something for everyone in a typical family to enjoy. Focusing on family values can also stimulate memories in adult family members, which can make them more likely to buy something that they can share with their own family. Kids can be a big target for marketers, as kids are usually the center of most families. Marketing products as "kid friendly" can be a great selling point for getting a whole family to buy in. Depending on what you're selling, see if you can work in a kid-friendly version to help boost sales.

Pique Their Interest and Make Them "Discover" Something. Many people think of things such as outer space or foreign lands when it comes to the word "discovery." Who makes discoveries every day? Usually just scientists, researchers and active readers. However, for the little-name consumer, a discovery can be a breath of fresh air from the boredom of everyday life. Additionally, when a consumer discovers something about a product or service, they are more likely to tell others about it, which can give your company some free word-of-mouth marketing. When a person discovers something, it also helps them feel smarter, which in turn can boost one's self-esteem. Discoveries for a consumer often come in the form of a new idea or a new and improved way to get things done. If your product or service falls into the category of something that is helpful to your consumer and/or it can benefit their life, this can be a good way to market it. Use key words that promote a change that can happen in the consumers' life. "New" is a keyword that often works well and piques interest.

Promote Fun and Laughter. Life can be very boring without some fun, games and humor. As the popular sayings go, "life is too short" and "laughter is the best medicine." Consumers are often looking for ways to have fun so if you market your product or service in a way that promotes a good time, you may have an upper advantage. Promoting your product or service as "fun" is also a good way to help eliminate boredom from your consumers' lives. Even if your product is not really "fun", there are still ways to integrate fun into it. For example, you could create a small flash game to put on your website about your product or service to promote the concept of fun. Another idea is to give your product a humorous name or do something that goes against the norm. You could also make your product interactive. For example, if you were manufacturing different BBQ sauces, you could make your labels "scratch and sniff" to let consumers smell the flavor before they even taste it.

Market Your Product as Scarce. When your product or service is hard to get, there is usually a higher demand. Scarcity often translates to exclusive. Consumers tend to pay top dollar for something that is unique and not easily accessible. If everyone has it, the demand may not be as high. Use keywords such as "last chance" or "if you don't buy it now," to create a sense of scarcity.

Romance and Sex Sells. As the old saying goes, "sex sells", because it invokes such a powerful emotion in consumers. Humans possess a powerful desire to be loved and to love. Though men and women interpret this in different ways (women tend to love the emotional, affectionate aspect and men tend to love the sexual aspect), romance and sex serve as a great selling point in marketing. It is important to remember not to be too over-the-top when it comes to using sex and romance. Don't give it all away, but invoke peoples' curiosities and fantasies, so to speak.

Market in Terms of Self-Expression. As a part of self-achievement, consumers often express themselves through products. For example, Red Bull once had the slogan "it gives you wings," which was meant to signify energy, strength, endurance and a high athletic ability. Consumers who wanted to see themselves in that light would decide to drink that product. Similarly, people who drive expensive cars may see themselves as successful and people who think of themselves as entrepreneurial may wear expensive clothes.

Use the Desire for Self-Improvement to Your Advantage. Humans are often changing and "reinventing" themselves in some way. To your advantage as a business owner, the world is always changing, which leads to a change in living. If your product or service can serve as a self-improvement tool in some way, use it to your advantage. Make your consumers feel powerful enough to take that first step towards a new or better life. Present yourself as a coach or an expert who is ready to support the consumer in any way possible, and then be sure to back this up with hard work and research! Don't forget to work goals into the mix, as goals often motivate most consumers.

Target Their Self-Esteem. Self-esteem is a big selling point in consumer psychology. Everybody wants to feel good about themselves and many people try to achieve that status by buying things that make them feel prestigious and important. Good marketing can be achieved by targeting your consumer's self-esteem needs—mostly the desire to fit in and sit high on the totem pole. To market your product or service as "elite" or "prestigious," there are a few things you will need to do beforehand. First, your business must stand out from all the rest in its industry. Your consumers have to perceive you as better than the rest because they will not have any problem paying more money for something that they think is more high-end. Secondly, don't underprice yourself. A lot of people who are just starting out think they can get more business by underpricing themselves and looking more affordable. However, it tends to be true that people get what they pay for and many people are willing to pay a higher price for something that they perceive to be of higher quality. Another point to consider is to take advantage of your product's aesthetics. Consumers go crazy over gold logos, high-end fabrics, and exquisite designs, because it allows them to show-off.

Save Them Time. Time is precious and there are only so many hours in a day. If you can market your product or service in a way that can save consumers time, you may have a powerful selling point. If your product or service can make the lives of your consumer more efficient, you absolutely cannot forget to make that known. When it comes to actually marketing your product, see if you can show your consumer just how easy it will be for them to save time and energy with your product or service. Try to bring together different aspects of life that take up time by marketing your product in a way that will accomplish two tasks at once. Focus on any aspect that can save your consumer time, steps, organization, or anything else that takes up a part of the day.

Knowledge is Power. The desire to be smart and knowledgeable is another hot spot where you can market your product or service to consumers. Humans believe that the more they know, the better decisions they can make and that is why knowledge is in high demand. If your product or service is not something that can help consumers learn something, you can still use this strategy to your advantage. Lay off the "selling" and just focus on informing your customer. This can help build trust between you and the customer and it makes the customer feel a lot more confident in his or her purchase. Make sure your website and any other content platform is well-written and contains informative information. You can also use seminars and webinars to further educate your prospective and current consumers.

Chapter 4: How To Be Successful With Social Media Marketing

Modern technology has brought marketing to a whole new level, especially with social media. Social media consists of powerful platforms, including Facebook, YouTube and Twitter among many more, all of which can be used to build your brand, establish your authority and connect with millions of consumers around the world. With the potential to reach people on an international level, social media marketing can help you expand your customer base and spread the word about your product or service with very little cost. According to the 2011 Social Media Marketing Industry report, small business owners are seeing the greatest results from this type of marketing. Social media marketing is also a great way to reduce marketing costs and become more efficient.

One of the most interesting things about social media marketing is that it opens up the potential to connect with your consumers on a personal level. Social media platforms allow you to personally express your thoughts, feelings and ideas with your audience. For example, you could write a status on your Facebook page about the development of your upcoming product or you could pass along an informative article along with your opinion.

Here are some more ideas that you can use to boost your presence on social media:

- Share your thoughts on your industry.

- Write about your own success stories or share the success stories of your past clients.

- Identify and address with your audiences' passion.

- Identify and address a problem that your audience has.

- Identify and address a fear of your audience.

- Build personal relationships through commenting and private messaging.

- Establish trust

Popular Social Media Platforms and How To Use Them For Marketing

Facebook. Facebook has more than one billion active users, the majority of them from the United States. About 600 million of those people use Facebook on their mobile device. The median Facebook user age is 22. Besides having your own personal profile, you can also make a page for a business, company, product, etc. Many businesses and companies have created multiple Facebook pages to reach out to their target market audience.

- Factors to consider
  - Profile Picture
    - Big profile pictures help the page stand out more. It is also the first thing that people will see, so it should be engaging and interesting.
  - Friends
    - It is good to reward loyal supporters of your page. For example, you can encourage them to share and like your page and then give them a shout-out on your wall. This sort of attention is good and will keep people coming back. There are several ways to get friends. The admin of the page can invite people to like it, people can like it on their own, or you can invite people through email.
  - Wall
    - It is important to be active. Status updates allow for "real-time" communication with those on your friends list. Friends who like the page can also post things on your wall, making it a two-way interaction channel. There is also the option to take polls, have contests, etc.
  - Photos/Videos
    - Both the admin of the page and friends can upload photos and videos. Photos and videos help capture the attention of people and for some, they may learn more by watching a video rather than by reading. The tagging option allows friends to be associated with a certain photo or video and it will show up on their personal page, thus making more people likely to see it.
  - Groups
    - Being active in groups will bring more attention to your Facebook page. For example, if you are active in a forum that is related to the product/business that your page is promoting, most people who are in that group are likely to check it out since they can relate to it. Groups also present a good opportunity to use incentives. For example, if you are offering something on your page it may be a good idea to mention that to people in the group so they can check it out.
  - Events
    - Your page can send out event notices to invite people to something such as a seminar or gathering. You can either send out event invitations to anyone who is on your page's friend list or you can enter somebody's email address manually. The great thing about Facebook events is that it will remind those who are attending the event about its occurrence usually a day before it happens. An event

invitation compiles all of the necessary information that people will need such as the time and location of the event and you can also add pictures to make it more personable.

Pinterest. Pinterest is a popular image-sharing website where you can find images and content of almost anything. While it may seem like just another trendy social media platform on the outside, it can actually be very useful for marketing your business. Many businesses like to share inspirational quotes, motivational pictures, or informative content such as recipes or projects on this site. However, there are a few things that not many people know about that you can use on Pinterest to your advantage.

- Factors consider
  - Videos
    - In addition to sharing images, you can also share videos that are uploaded to YouTube and Vimeo. By pinning any videos you have on those platforms, you can expose them to a whole new set of people and possibly gain more leads. You will also likely see a boost in plays.
    - To pin a video, simply go to that video on its host website and look for the pin button under the sharing options.
  - Podcasts
    - You can also upload podcasts, which are perfect for consumers who spend great amounts of time doing something else, such as driving, cleaning or relaxing. You can post audio clips that are uploaded to the audio hosting website, SoundCloud.
    - While prospective consumers are not likely to listen to long podcasts on this website, a good idea is to post a short clip from a podcast and have it serve as a preview. Then direct them to where they can listen to the entire clip.
    - Don't forget to pin an image with your sound clip, as graphics and visuals are twice as likely to capture and hold peoples' attention.
  - Get a Business Page
    - Recently, Pinterest added a "business page" option for business owners. A business page will provide you information such as unique page visits, number of re-pins, popular content and other useful analytics.
  - Create Boards that are Related To Your Business
    - With Pinterest, it is easy to categorize the content you pin by creating different boards. It is a good idea to have about 30% of your content be directly related to your business. Break up the rest of your content by trying to appeal to your target audience.

For example, here are a couple of Pinterest boards I have created: Health and Self Improvement.

For more advanced information on how to use Facebook to market and make money with your business, be sure to check out my best-selling book: Facebook: The Top 100 Best Ways To Use Facebook For Business, Marketing, & Making Money.

LinkedIn. LinkedIn is a popular social media website for professionals, connecting over 65 million people each year. Most of those with profiles on LinkedIn have influence over decisions made in their company. It is a free and very useful website in social media marketing. It is very similar to Facebook in the way it is set up. For example, you can post a status on your LinkedIn profile just as you can on your Facebook profile. However, LinkedIn focuses more on businesses and companies and allowing their employees to connect on a professional yet personal level.

- Factors to consider
  - Groups
    - You can make your group more likely to appear in searches by using specific keywords that pertain to the group. It will even make it more likely to show up in Google. Groups are also helpful in directing more traffic to your actual website. You can use the RSS feed to have your blog posts automatically updated within the group. Since people find the group by looking for certain keywords, it is likely that you can connect to those people in terms of what your business provides.
  - Events
    - The events option on LinkedIn is like Facebook Events but much more powerful. Once a person confirms that they are attending an event, everyone on their list can see it so your event can possibly go viral.
    - Advanced Search
      - You can run an advanced search on LinkedIn to find those who fall in your target market audience. With advanced search, you can find people by putting in specific industry, title, company, etc. Keywords. Once you find these people, you can personally connect with them by sending them a private message.

Twitter. Twitter is a micro-blogging website and it allows both individuals and businesses to post brief messages that can be seen worldwide. There are over 100 million registered Twitter users in the United States. These brief messages are known as "tweets" and are limited to 140 characters. Your friends on this site are called your "followers." Using Twitter for social media marketing is an inbound marketing strategy and very powerful!

- Steps to Marketing on Twitter
  - Use your personal name or business name in order to make a professional appearance and to brand yourself.
  - Follow other targeted users who may be interested in your business in order to get them to follow you back. This helps build your target market audience.
  - You can promote your Twitter page on other pages such as Facebook, LinkedIn, and your personal website.
  - Since there is a 140 character limit, Twitter is good for sending out short announcements, such as a discounted product or a new video or blog. You can also ask questions of your followers and stimulate interaction that way.
  - You can "retweet" a post from another user or business to build on your product of service.

There is a lot more that you can do with Twitter, for more advanced information on how you can use Twitter to successfully market your business, be sure to check out my book: Twitter: How To Market & Make Money With Twitter.

YouTube. Youtube is probably the best known video-hosting website, where people upload all kinds of useful and helpful videos. It is important for every business to have a YouTube account, because no matter how much written content you pass around, there will always be consumers who enjoy learning through seeing and hearing rather than reading. The best thing about YouTube is that it is easy to set up. Here are some more ways that you can use YouTube to your advantage:

- Factors to consider
  - Channels
    - Set your brand by customizing your channel. You can give your channel a title and that is how people can search for you. Your title and your username do not have to match. You can set the background color of your channel or upload your own background, you can choose which videos will be featured on your channel's homepage and you can choose your own avatar. You can also provide a written description for your channel. By making the description search-engine optimized, it will be more likely to show up in search-engine results.
  - Tags
    - By adding tags to both your channel and your videos, it will increase the likeliness that people will find your videos. Tags are

one word descriptions that are related to the information in the video or the channel.

- ◦ Video Hosting
  - ▪ Each uploaded video has a space for a description of the video. That space can be used to tell what the video is about, to transcribe the video, or to give links directing viewers to more information.
- ◦ Subscribers
  - ▪ You can have subscribers on YouTube. When a person chooses to subscribe to your channel, any video that you post will automatically show up on the subscriber's homepage every time they log-in to YouTube.

Blogs. Blogs are a great way to keep your audience entertained, informed and attracted. Most businesses have a blog on their website where consumers can learn more about the business and its products/services. Remember how important it is to make consumers feel smart? Here are some tips for making a blog Appealing to Readers:

1. **Make a good first impression.** People visit blogs in order to learn something or find a solution to their problems, so it is important to stay on topic and be concerned about the reader. This will make them eager to keep coming back for more and they may even pass the link on to others. If the reader requests information, make sure that they receive it, otherwise they will start to look elsewhere.

2. **Create a Unique Presence/Brand.** One important feature to consider is the design of your blog. Using a free template will not make your blog stand out from the millions of others that are out there. It may be worth the money to even spend a few dollars on a nice, clean, elegant design. Even if the design costs $5 or more, it is more likely than not to stand out and get noticed. If you are not an expert on blogs or web design, this is a good time to outsource this job to a professional. My favorite place to do this is: www.Odesk.com and www.Elance.com. For more advanced information on outsourcing, be sure to check out my book on: Team Building.

3. **Choose a Professional Logo and Tagline.** By having a professional logo, your blog will be more recognizable and come off as more professional. Readers in the blog community will know what your blog is about just by seeing the logo. The tagline is also important because, similar to a tweet, it lets readers know about the blog in a couple of words and is also important for keywords that are related to the topic of the blog. This can be done very inexpensively at www.Fiverr.com.

4. **Content is Key.** The content on your blog is what is going to attract readers and traffic, especially people who like to learn information through reading.

5. **Interact with Similar Bloggers.** Chances are there are bloggers who are writing about the same or similar subject somewhere out there. By becoming friends with them and supporting each other's blog, it will heighten the chances of getting the word out there about your own blog. This is similar to networking.

Tips for Driving Traffic to a Blog

1. Use blog aggregators to drive more traffic (example alltop.com). These sites pair you're most recent entry to a category and help people find what they are looking for.

2. Use blog directories as well.

3. Write guest blogs. "Guest blogging is the act of writing for another blog, with the hope of getting quality back-links, getting traffic, gaining exposure and building relationships." The only downside of guest blogging is that you are giving away your information for free, but in return you may gain more traffic and subscribers that will benefit the blog and your business in the long term.

4. Be active in forums and direct people to your blog or leave a link to your blog in your signature of each post.

5. You should also allow others to make guest posts on your own blog since that can also increase traffic.

6. Be consistent in your posts. Research shows that blogs that update continuously get more traffic than blogs that only post here and there.

7. Optimize your blog for mobile devices since many people connect online with their iPhone, smartphone, or tablet.

8. Blog about current issues and top news to gain readers' attention.

9. Create an email list so you can have subscribers. The earlier you start this the better. It is a long term process but can pay huge dividends in the long run!

Instagram. Similar to Pinterest, Instagram is another image-sharing website. The difference is that it is much more casual and personal. Users upload pictures with hashtags that categorize the picture and they can even experiment with different "filters" which can change the color and overall feel of the image. While not many businesses may think of Instagram as a marketing platform, it can actually be a great way to spread a brand.

- Factors to consider:
  - Photo Contests
    - A great way to encourage fan engagement is to hold photo contests. With photo contests, you can ask users to upload a certain kind of picture and tag it with a # that represents your brand. For example, Sony held an Instagram photo contest about love. The company invited fans to post pictures of something that symbolized love to them and tag it with #SonyX. Then the company would pick a winner every day.
  - Showcasing
    - Another good idea for businesses is to showcase your customers by taking pictures of them using your product or service and posting it on Instagram. You can pair this with a customer success story and then tag it with your brand. When you see someone similar to yourself succeeding with a business, it makes you more likely to use that business yourself.

When you manage multiple social media platforms, it can be challenging to keep track of what's going on with every single one. A really good idea is to use automated software that will post to your social media platforms on your behalf. Buffer is a really good one that posts to Twitter, Facebook, LinkedIn and Google+ all at once. It is hard to find automation software that can also post to YouTube, Pinterest, Instagram and your blog, but even if you just use a program like Buffer to cover Facebook, Twitter and LinkedIn, you will have more time to manually manage the other sites.

One really useful idea is to set up a marketing calendar. It doesn't have to be anything fancy, just a basic outline of what you're going to post, where and on what day. It also comes in handy when planning for trends, such as major holidays or major events.

Chapter 5: The Best Sales Techniques for Marketing

Marketing would not be marketing without sales. Marketing is just one piece of the puzzle... it attracts customers so that you can sell to them. You as a business owner must orchestrate the two so that your business flourishes. This chapter will help you discover some of the best strategies for selling so that you can close more deals and win more customers.

Tips on Preparing Yourself For Working in Sales

1. Prepare yourself for rejection, because like or not, it is going to happen. Closing a sale with 100% of your clients is simply impossible. Some consumers just don't want to be bothered with sales pitches, especially if it's done through a cold-call or a random approach. However, that's not to say that those approaches can't get you leads, new customers and some word-of-mouth marketing. Preparing yourself for rejection is important because you cannot avoid it and it is something you will have to overcome in order to be successful. Rejection is hard to get over because it's such an awful feeling and many people fear it. However, overcoming that fear can be easier than you may think. Start by telling yourself that life is full of fears and that you've gotten past many before. Think about some times when you were fearful and how you overcame it. Another good idea is to research the art of selling so you go into it with some knowledge and a game plan.

2. Eliminate your doubts and learn how to catch yourself when you start making excuses for not being a good seller. While it is natural to doubt yourself and make excuses sometimes, it is important to not let it take charge of your career. Here is some very important advice—if you want to succeed at something, it has to come from within. You have to want it. If you continuously tell yourself that you will succeed in sales, then you will. If you keep making excuses for yourself, you will not succeed. This can be a challenge for the majority of people but with a little bit of personal development, you can do it.

3. Practice daily self-discipline measures. Without self-discipline, it can be easy to get caught up and distracted by your emotions or other things that are going on in your life. Self-discipline will help you keep your focus despite anything that comes up. Most small business owners have a lot of flexibility in their schedule, so it is very easy to put things off. That's where you have to get serious. Make sure you practice self-discipline and become serious about your career, where it's going and how you will get through your days. The best strategy is to do the most important thing

first, no matter how hard it is and then focus on the other miscellaneous tasks that can be done much easier and at a later time.

4. Be yourself and try to sell to like-minded people. Consumers are more likely to make purchases from someone who they like. The better you can master your likeability, the more likely you are to make good impressions and get more sales. Try and find things in common, give a compliment here and there and don't forget to flash a genuine smile to help the transaction go smoothly.

5. Learn from your mistakes because that is the best way to learn. Nobody is a born salesperson and it will take you some trial and error until you find a technique that works best for you. Failure can be hard to accept because nobody likes to mess up, but it is inevitable—the best way to learn how to embrace failure is to remind yourself how great you are. Think about past situations in which you've learned from your mistakes and find some inspiration there.

6. Be passionate about your business and product. If you don't care about what you're doing and what you're selling, your consumers will be able to sense that. The good news is that most people get into business because they *are* passionate about something. Still, it is very possible to lose that passion quickly, so always keep yourself in check with what you're doing.

7. Push yourself to keep going until you get to the top! Motivate yourself to become the best in your industry. You will have to want it to get there; you won't make it by just waiting for a good opportunity to come along. Always remember that hard work pays off! This is shown nicely in one of my favorite speeches from Arnold Schwarzenegger: The Six Secrets To Success.

8. Work with your customer to find the root cause of their problem. The real problem is what you're trying to solve as a salesperson. The idea is to figure out what their issue is and then sell your product or service in a way that will solve the issue. It's not always as simple as the problem your customer tells you, either. This is why it is important to know how to communicate and engage in conversation with your customer. You want to make sure that you're going to treat the right problem. The better you can solve the problem, the more likely that customer is to do repeat business with you. A good way to lose a customer for life is to sell them something they don't need and for them to find out they had a better option later on!

9. Don't flat out tell your customer why they should buy something from you. Instead, present the facts and then let him or her come to that conclusion by themselves. Think about it—most people have an instinct in them where they don't like it when other people tell them what to do. Would

you want someone to tell you what to do? It is a much more natural process to let the customers make the decision for themselves. Focus more on presenting the facts and catering to their needs to increase the likelihood that your customer says yes to the sale.

10. Be aware of how much talking you do. It may seem natural to do all the talking when you're the salesperson, but don't forget about the importance of your customer. Make sure they ask questions and make sure that you listen to those questions intently. Don't talk so much that your customer feels unimportant or unable to ask enough questions to come to a decision.

11. While it is important to present facts to your consumer, don't try to over-educate right away. The first focus will always be on the problem. Once you and your consumer know the problem, then go ahead and start talking about the facts and how your product can help them.

12. Never try to read the mind of your consumer. Sometimes making an assumption can actually damage the relationship and make you look too eager to sell. The key is to ask questions and be straightforward.

13. Always be open and honest with your consumers. It is almost like the same thing as lying—the truth often comes out anyway and it makes you look bad. Remember the old saying, "honesty is the best policy." Being honest can also help you build relationships that are solid and full of trust.

14. Use props. Although this may seem a little over-the-top, props really do have a lasting effect on your consumer. Props are a really good way to capture attention when attention may be slipping. If you've ever seen the movie Napoleon Dynamite, think about when Uncle Rico was making a career out of being a Tupperware salesman. In one scene, he is trying to sell the Tupperware to a couple and they start to look uninterested. Then he suddenly pulls out a large model of a Viking ship and suddenly re-captures their attention, ultimately closing the sale.

15. Don't be afraid to upsell. Many people shy away from upselling because they think the consumer will just brush it off as another way to get money. Upselling is a common and surprisingly easy way to get a little more out of your customer. Fast food restaurants upsell all the time when they ask, "Do you want to go for a large size for JUST 25 cents more!?" Most of the time, you'll just say, "Yeah sure." See how easy that was?

16. Make sure you do some price comparisons. Pricing your product can be tricky. You don't want to undercut yourself in an attempt to make more sales. If you do that, people might think your product is low-quality because it is so cheap. While I have seen companies successfully do this, it can be a huge risk. On the other hand, you don't want to over-price your products and services either because then consumers will just go to your

competitors. Instead, do some shopping around and settle on a fair price that is not too low, not too high but appealing enough to get sales. A good way to start is by doing some market research.

17. Create a customer rewards program. It doesn't have to be anything crazy, but customers like to be rewarded and that can make them loyal buyers. Some companies do a promotion where their customer gets something free or discounted on their birthday. Other companies do monthly specials. Some do points that can be accumulated over time. The way to do it is completely up to you, but don't miss out on this opportunity.

18. If possible, give away a few free samples. It may be a bit costly at first but it helps consumers build trust in you. A free sample can be as simple as giving away a few free book chapters or giving away a small version of a product. Many lawyers and accountants give out free first consultations so their clients can get a feel for what's going on. That usually leads to a commitment.

19. If possible, test out your product or service with a "local" audience and then go bigger if it hits off. This can help you save money, especially if you're just starting out. If you can make a hit with a small audience, think about the possibilities when you reach out to a larger audience.

20. All in all, keep it professional. Consumers buy from "professional" companies. How many times have you seen a customer complaint about something where the person goes, "...and that was not professional at all!"

Chapter 6: Marketing Secrets That Help Drive Sales & Profit

Now that you have some great ideas on how you want to market your product, it's time to discover even more marketing secrets that you can implement into your business in order to close more deals. Remember, successful marketing will take some time as well as some experimenting, so don't be afraid to just start somewhere and keep going until you've found the ultimate formula. At the end of this chapter, you will find a great marketing plan where you can put it all together to get started.

1. Put your social media handle on everything—business cards, advertisements, handouts and even at the end of any videos you make. The more you can spread your handles, the more likely it will be that people look at your social media platforms and follow you.

2. Use popular, themed hashtags such as #FlashbackFriday to engage with your audience. Trending hashtags are the best to aim for because those are what people are actively searching for. The more popular the hashtag, the more likely you are to achieve audience engagement.

3. Use plenty of visuals in your marketing campaigns and always link them to your home website to drive traffic and boost sales.

4. Keep an eye on the social media websites of your competitors. Watching them can give you some great ideas.

5. Don't forget about offline marketing tactics such as sales letters, newspaper ads, brochures and even billboards. Not everyone is always online and some people may not even have access to a computer, so these types of marketing are still valuable.

6. On social media, host photo and video contests. This is a good way to increase audience engagement by letting people share a part of their own lives while also engaging with you.

7. Ask your audience for opinions and allow them to cast votes, either online (the most popular and easy way) or offline in a mailed survey. This can help make your consumers feel like their opinion matters and that can help build trust. It can also give you great ideas on how you can improve your product or service.

8. Another good idea is to hold caption contests online. This can allow your audience to get creative and share their ideas with you. It also helps attract more people to your page to read the various captions.

9. If possible, hold a giveaway event every so often where you randomly give away your product or service for free to a lucky winner. This is a good way to get the word out about your business and instead of monetary compensation, you could get a good review and that person can potentially spread the word about you.

10. Cross-market on all social media platforms that you have. A good idea is to link them all together using a third-party software and post directly from that platform. Different people use different platforms so the more you post on each one, the more people you can reach.

11. Study your audience. Get inside of their head. Figure out what words, phrases and visuals you need to use to capture their attention and make them interested in you. This is the best way to make sure that you stay on top in your industry.

12. Create your own infographics and pass them around online. Not only are infographics informative but they also serve as shareable content.

13. Learn how to properly set up your website to attract the most people. Make sure you use big headings to catch your readers' eyes and post helpful testimonials that will make consumers feel more comfortable buying from you. Don't forget to make your contact information available and easy to find. Including a "call to action" can also be helpful for motivating buyers.

14. Strategically use statistics in your marketing tactics. Consumers trust in statistics and they can really influence whether or not someone buys your product or service. For example, if you're selling a product that could benefit senior citizens, try to find a statistic that can go with it. For example, if you're marketing a blender to senior citizens, try to find a statistic that says something like "85% of senior citizens state that meal time is easier when they make smoothies."

15. If you're an expert in your field, make it known! Show how well you know your industry by talking about it in detail, setting up a specific blog for it, post articles, statistics, etc. When consumers can tell that you know what you're talking about, it makes you come off as trusting and professional. They will feel more comfortable in how you stand in your industry.

16. Write helpful articles or blogs (or at least have a ghostwriter write them for you). This is a great way to help you come off as an expert in your field. For example, if you're selling a special kind of blender, you could provide articles on smoothie recipes, how-to articles on how to clean and care for blenders, etc. Always write your articles in a fashion that will inform and help your audience and always make it about your product or service. Some businesses are afraid that how-to articles and tutorials will defer

consumers from needing their help, but many people end up coming to the business for more help or services.

17. If you're selling multiple but similar products, make sure you include a product comparison chart on your website or sales brochure. This can answer any questions that consumers may have and help them decide which product to buy. If you don't offer a comparison, you may actually overwhelm your consumer with decisions and they might decide to buy from a different business.

18. Link your content together. For example, if you have multiple articles, link to another, related article at the bottom. This can encourage your consumers to read on and learn more about you and your product or service. A good and easy way to do this is to write something like, "Click here to read more about [insert topic here]."

19. If you're looking to build your email list, find a program that allows a pop-up to appear on your website asking consumers to join your newsletter or email list. This idea can often be controversial, as many people find those pop-ups annoying, but the research shows that they don't hurt sales and they dramatically help in building your mailing list.

20. Write (or get a ghostwriter to write) an eBook related to your industry or product/service and offer it to your consumers. You can give it away for free to try and build your email list or to get consumers excited about your business. You could also give it away with a purchase or just sell it on its own. Consumers like getting informative freebies and they often like to read more on what they're getting and an ebook can be a great way to get that information through to them. If you sell it, it also serves as an additional source of income.

21. Write articles that are aimed toward beginners or newbies. These articles can be very informative and give your consumer more information, thus answering any frequently asked questions they may have. It can ease the level of trust and comfort they have with your business and it may increase the chances of a sale. Not many businesses do this so it is definitely a great idea to follow-up on.

22. Make sure your articles and other written content are worthy of reading. Material that is quickly thrown together, unedited or too vague often gets trashy reviews and it doesn't make you appear professional. If writing is your weak spot, invest in a ghostwriter or a professional editor. It will be well worth the money. All too often a consumer says, "If their writing is this bad, imagine how bad their product or service is!"

23. Let your personality shine through in all of your content—videos, articles, etc. Don't make yourself sound like a textbook. Try to be conversational,

friendly and engaging. You are twice as likely to hold readers' and watchers' attention. Pretend that you're in a college lecture—who would you rather listen to, the monotone professor or the one who is walking back and forth, changing their tone, using gestures, etc.?

24. To reach even more consumers, experiment with recording a podcast. Podcasts are perfect for people who are always on the road. Offer your podcasts as free downloads so they can listen to your podcast in their car.

25. Don't be afraid to collaborate with other people in your industry. At first it may feel like you're just giving your business away for free, but in reality, it can actually drive your sales high. For example, I know a freelance writer who is very popular and in demand but she only has enough time to take on a few clients at a time. She likes to keep a few other writer contacts in her book so that she can refer them to anyone who comes to her with a job that she can't take. It sounds like losing business, but it can actually be a great relationship builder because when *those* writers can't take on a job, they refer clients to *her*. You can also exchange knowledge with other people in your industry as well. If both people are acting in good faith, then this can really help your business out in a variety of ways! You can even form a small group of people, known as the mastermind group, to keep each other accountable and to exchange ideas and experiences. You will be much more effective working as a group then you will be all by yourself.

26. Create a schedule for posting your content and make it consistent. Do not post everything at once or you can overwhelm or bore your consumers. Keep it fresh and not too often. One good idea is to make a new blog post once a week or even once a month. If you build up a following, those followers will catch on to your schedule and know when to check back for new content.

27. Make sure your website is optimized for mobility. Many consumers surf the web on their phones now and if a website is not optimized for the tiny screen, it can cause you to miss out on traffic. It can be a little expensive to do this sometimes, but well worth it in the long term!

28. Study other businesses that are successful and use them as your model. Don't copy their style or content but try to find a pattern that they use and see if you can emulate that. If that business is successful with it, odds are, you can be too. It also can help you find the inspiration for new ideas.

29. Pay close attention to the headlines and titles you use on your blogs and articles. Take the time to come up with good ones that catch attention and really stand out.

30. Establish a strong customer service department and emphasize that to your consumers. Think back to the last time you dealt with a company that had poor customer service—how frustrated were you? You probably swore up and down that you'd never buy from them again. Don't let that happen to you! Consumers really do appreciate genuine customer service.

Marketing Action Plan

This is where you put it all together and start coming up with your ideal plan for marketing to your customer base. Be sure to prepare yourself mentally and try to eliminate negative thoughts and fears before diving in! Now take a piece of paper and pen and write down 10 negative emotions or excuses that you are feeling towards your business (be honest with yourself, no one will see this but you):

Writing these down will help you become more aware of the situation, but most importantly, it gives you control. Now that you have these negative thoughts and feelings in front of you, say some positive affirmations to counter each of the ten negative emotions or excuses you just wrote down. This will help you to escape that negative mindset and jump into the marketer's mindset.

Next, brainstorm some answers to these questions:

1. What is my brand? How will I present my brand?

2. How can I give my brand a personal touch?

3. How can I get consumers to become a "fan" of me and my business?

4. What will I do for customer service that can stand out from other businesses in my industry?

5. Am I an expert in my field? How can I present myself as an expert to build trust with my audience?

Once you've answered those questions, begin to think about figuring out your target market audience. Here are the questions from chapter 2 that you can focus on answering:

- Who am I targeting?

- What am I selling to these targets?

- Where are my targets located?

- When will I approach my targets?

- Why would my targets be interested in my business?

- How will I reach my targets?

Focus on all those aspects until you start to get a nice idea of how you want to attract target customers and sales. Once you've made a few sales and acquired a few followers, the next step is to develop your ideal customer profile. To develop your ideal customer profile, take a handful of your best customers and try to construct a profile from the traits of those customers. Think about demographics, socioeconomic factors and personality traits.

Also, make a list of the ways you plan on advertising your product or service. Flip back a few pages to remind yourself of all the different kinds of advertising. Remember, advertising is not the same as marketing but you will need some form of advertising to start spreading the word about your business. Once you've made your list, start thinking about more specific marketing strategies. Go back to chapter 3 and look through the list to see if you can match any with your business.

Next, start to think about social media marketing. What platforms do you have a business presence on? Will you need to create accounts on new platforms? Remember, you don't need to have an account on every single social media platform—think about which ones can serve your business and industry the best. Don't be afraid to experiment with each platform to see which one's you get the most response on. For now, pick one platform to master and then begin to master the other ones in the future.

Finally, start to prepare yourself for the sales process—the most important part of the game. Brush up on your sales skills by referring to chapter 5. I would say the best place to start is to build up your communication skills, as those are an essential skill set that you will need when dealing with people. Mentally prepare yourself to escape the "sleazy salesman" stereotype and transform yourself into a unique salesperson who everyone likes so that you can capitalize on your marketing efforts.

Conclusion

I hope this book was able to give you some great ideas on how to successfully market your business so that you can reach more people, generate more sales and become more profitable.

The next step is to work on your action plan. Becoming a marketing master will definitely not happen overnight. It is something that you really need to work on and adjust over time. Just stay positive and realize that all of your hard work will surely pay off. Try and save yourself as much time and aggravation as possible by modeling successful companies or people. There is no "right" answer when it comes to marketing. You will need to experiment with different approaches and strategies before you can find the right strategies for your business. Lots of people have marketing degrees, but anyone can become an expert at marketing. Just remember to be passionate, determined, dedicated and motivated. Be sure to learn from your mistakes and keep pressing forward until you have found the strategies that work best for you and your business.

Finally, if you discovered at least one thing that has helped you or that you think would be beneficial to someone else, be sure to take a few seconds to easily post a quick positive review. As an author, your positive feedback is desperately needed. Your highly valuable five star reviews are like a river of golden joy flowing through a sunny forest of mighty trees and beautiful flowers! *To do your good deed in making the world a better place by helping others with your valuable insight, just leave a nice review.*

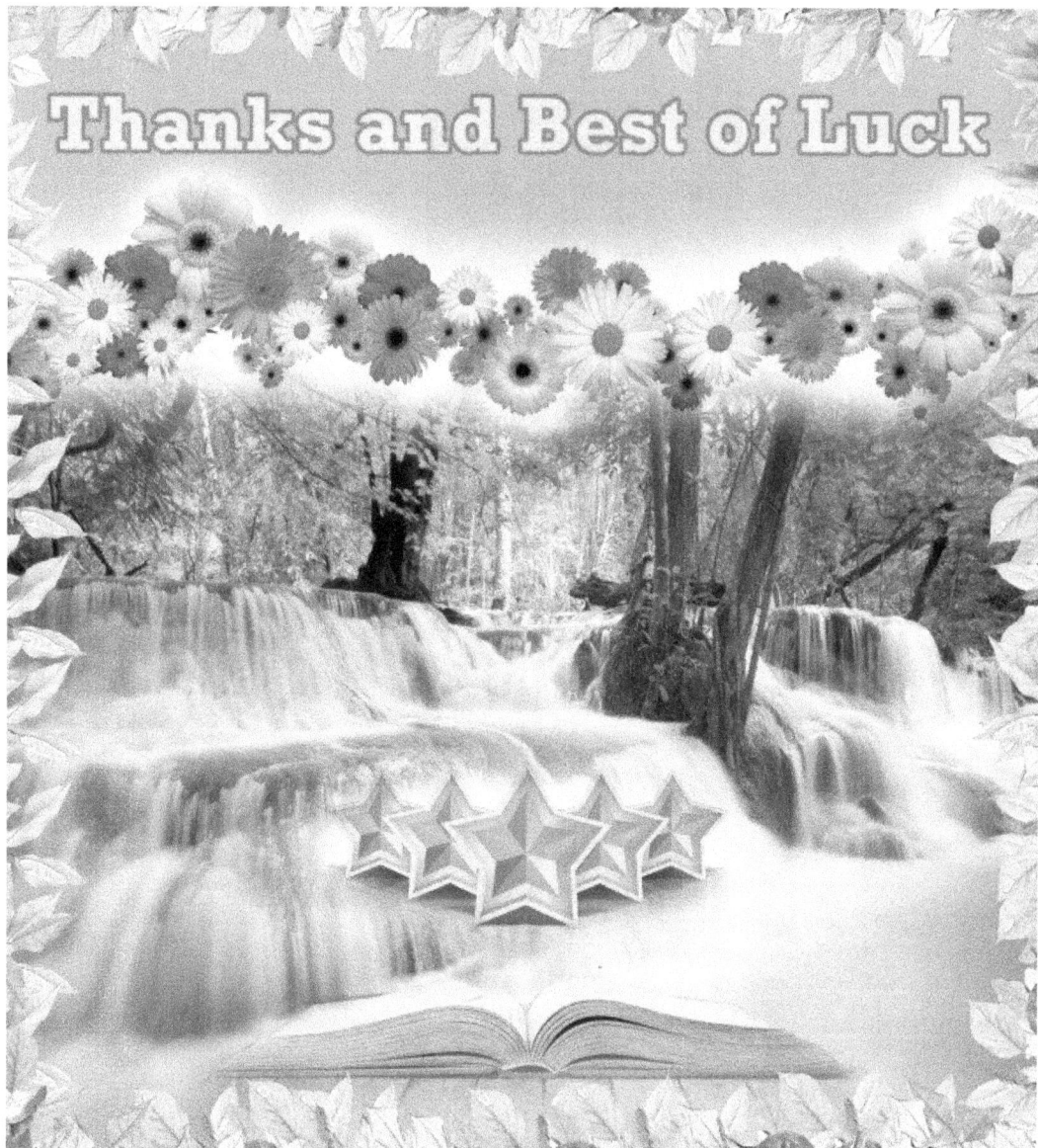

Thanks and Best of Luck

My Other Books and Audio Books

www.AcesEbooks.com

Business & Finance Books

LEADERSHIP

THE TOP 100 BEST WAYS
TO BE A GREAT LEADER

Ace McCloud

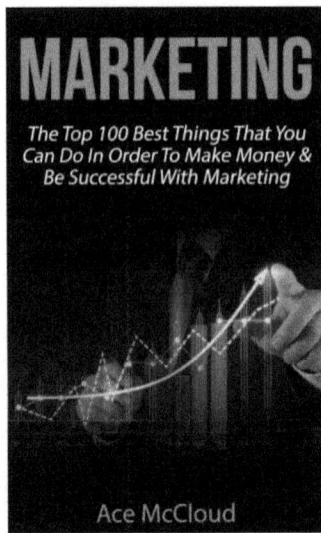

MARKETING

The Top 100 Best Things That You
Can Do In Order To Make Money &
Be Successful With Marketing

Ace McCloud

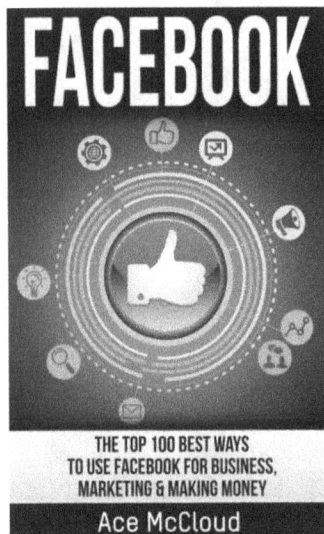

FACEBOOK

THE TOP 100 BEST WAYS
TO USE FACEBOOK FOR BUSINESS,
MARKETING & MAKING MONEY

Ace McCloud

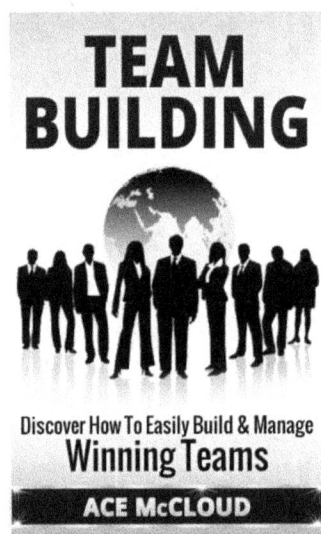

TEAM BUILDING

Discover How To Easily Build & Manage
Winning Teams

ACE McCLOUD

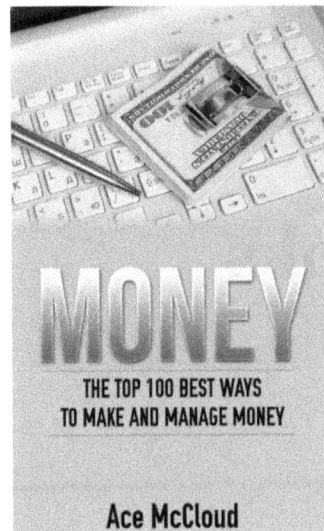

MONEY

THE TOP 100 BEST WAYS
TO MAKE AND MANAGE MONEY

Ace McCloud

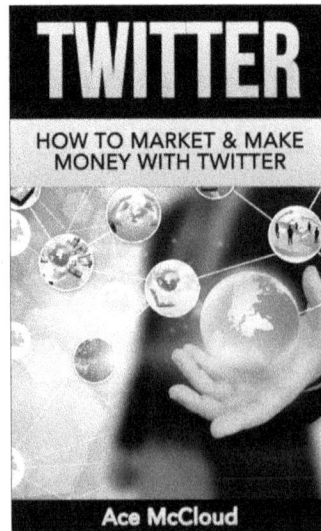

TWITTER

HOW TO MARKET & MAKE
MONEY WITH TWITTER

Ace McCloud

COMMUNICATION SKILLS

Discover The Best Ways To Communicate,
Be Charismatic, Use Body Language,
Persuade & Be A Great Conversationalist

Ace McCloud

YouTube

THE TOP 100 BEST WAYS
TO MARKET & MAKE MONEY WITH YOUTUBE

Ace McCloud

Peak Performance Books

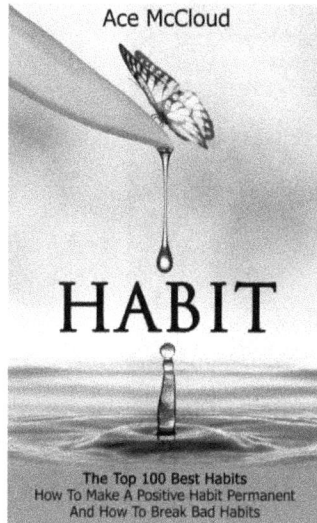

SUCCESS
SUCCESS STRATEGIES
THE TOP 100 BEST WAYS TO BE SUCCESSFUL

Ace McCloud

Ace McCloud

HABIT

The Top 100 Best Habits
How To Make A Positive Habit Permanent
And How To Break Bad Habits

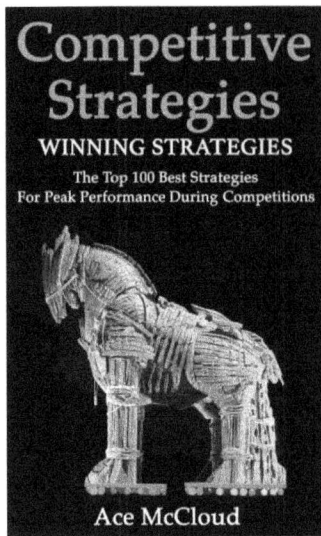

Be sure to check out my audio books as well!

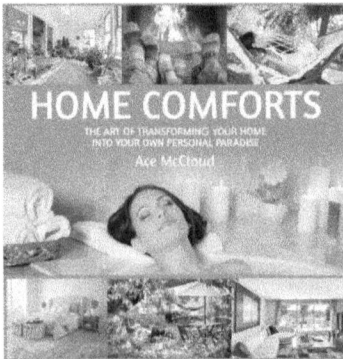

Check out my website at: **www.AcesEbooks.com** for a complete list of all of my books and high quality audio books. I enjoy bringing you the best knowledge in the world and wish you the best in using this information to make your journey through life better and more enjoyable! **Best of luck to you!**